WALK TO FREEDOM

MONTGOMERY BUS BOYCOTT

Virginia Loh-Hagan

45TH PARALLEL PRESS

Published in the United States of America by Cherry Lake Publishing
Ann Arbor, Michigan
www.cherrylakepublishing.com

Reading Adviser: Marla Conn, MS, Ed., Literacy specialist, Read-Ability Inc.
Cover Designer: Felicia Macheske

Photo Credits: © Savvapanf Photo/Shutterstock.com, cover, 1; © Library of Congress, LC-DIG-ppmsca-41027, 5;
© Everett Historical/Shutterstock.com, 6; © Library of Congress, LC-DIG-ppmsca-47894, 11; © Don Cravens/
Getty Images, 12; © Library of Congress, LC-DIG-ppmsc-00199, 17; © Library of Congress, LC-USZ62-122996, 18;
© PhotosmithInc/Shutterstock.com, 21; © Grey Villet/Getty Images, 22; © Grzegorz Burakovsky/Shutterstock.
com, 25; © Bettmann/Getty Images, 29

Graphic Elements Throughout: © Chipmunk131/Shutterstock.com; © Nowik Sylwia/Shutterstock.com;
© Andrey_Popov/Shutterstock.com; © NadzeyaShanchuk/Shutterstock.com; © KathyGold/Shutterstock.com;
© Black creator/Shutterstock.com; © Edvard Molnar/Shutterstock.com; © Elenadesign/Shutterstock.com;
© estherpoon/Shutterstock.com

45th Parallel Press is an imprint of Cherry Lake Publishing.

Library of Congress Cataloging-in-Publication Data

Names: Loh-Hagan, Virginia, author.
Title: Walk to freedom : Montgomery Bus Boycott / Virginia Loh-Hagan.
Description: Ann Arbor : Cherry Lake Publishing, [2020]. | Series: Behind the curtain | Includes index.
Identifiers: LCCN 2019032894 (print) | LCCN 2019032895 (ebook) | ISBN 9781534159464 (hardcover) |
    ISBN 9781534161764 (paperback) | ISBN 9781534160613 (pdf) | ISBN 9781534162914 (ebook)
Subjects: LCSH: Montgomery Bus Boycott, Montgomery, Ala., 1955-1956–Juvenile literature. | Montgomery
    (Ala.)–Race relations–Juvenile literature. | Segregation in transportation–Alabama–Montgomery–History–20th
    century–Juvenile literature. | African Americans–Civil rights–Alabama–Montgomery–History–20th century–
    Juvenile literature.
Classification: LCC F334.M79 L64 2020 (print) | LCC F334.M79 (ebook) | DDC 323.1196/073076147–dc23
LC record available at https://lccn.loc.gov/2019032894
LC ebook record available at https://lccn.loc.gov/2019032895

Cherry Lake Publishing would like to acknowledge the work of the Partnership for 21st Century Learning,
a Network of Battelle for Kids. Please visit *http://www.battelleforkids.org/networks/p21* for more information.

Printed in the United States of America
Corporate Graphics

A Note on Dramatic Retellings

Participating in Readers Theater, or dramatic retellings, can greatly improve reading skills, especially fluency. The books in the **BEHIND THE CURTAIN** series give readers opportunities to learn about important historical events in a fun and engaging way. These books serve as a bridge to more complex texts. All the characters are real figures from history; however, their stories have been fictionalized. To learn more about the people and the events, check out the Viewpoints and Perspectives series and the Perspectives Library series, as the **BEHIND THE CURTAIN** books are aligned to these stories.

TABLE of CONTENTS

HISTORICAL BACKGROUND

Claudette Colvin is an African American nurse. On March 2, 1955, she was arrested. She was 15 years old. She refused to give up her seat on the bus to a white woman.

Rosa Parks was an African American seamstress. On December 1, 1955, she refused to give up her seat to a white man. She was arrested.

These events happened in Montgomery, Alabama. They helped spark the Montgomery bus boycott. This boycott happened from December 5, 1955, to December 20, 1956. It was the first important U.S. protest against segregation. African Americans weren't treated fairly. They had to sit in the back of the bus. They didn't think this was fair. So, they fought for their civil rights.

Vocabulary

arrested (uh-REST-id) taken into custody for committing a crime

seamstress (SEEM-stris) a woman who sews

boycott (BOI-kaht) a ban

segregation (seg-rih-GAY-shuhn) system that keeps different groups separated

civil rights (SIV-uhl RITES) a citizen's rights to freedom and equality

FLASH FACT!

In the South, there were "colored only" areas.

Vocabulary

car pools (KAHR POOLZ)
sharing rides

integrated (IN-tuh-gray-tid)
racially mixed

illegal (ih-LEE-guhl)
against the law

African Americans in Montgomery organized. They formed the Montgomery Improvement Association (MIA). They elected Dr. Martin Luther King Jr. as their president. King became a national civil rights leader.

About 40,000 African Americans refused to ride the city buses in Montgomery. They organized car pools. African American cab drivers charged the same as buses. Many African Americans walked. They did what they could do to boycott the buses.

Montgomery's buses were integrated on December 21, 1956. The courts decided that segregated buses were illegal. The boycott lasted 381 days. It was an example of nonviolent protest. It brought national attention to the struggles of African Americans.

CAST of CHARACTERS

NARRATOR: person who helps tell the story

LOUIS WASHBURN: an African American civil rights activist

REGINALD BROWN: an African American church leader

ROSA PARKS: an African American civil rights activist who refused to give up her bus seat

MATILDA LEE: a white woman who is an **opponent** of the boycott

BACKSTORY
SPOTLIGHT BIOGRAPHY

Jo Ann Robinson was an African American woman. She was born in 1912. She moved to Montgomery, Alabama. She taught at Alabama State College. Soon after moving to Montgomery, she sat in the "whites only" section of the bus. A bus driver yelled at her. She never forgot about this. She became the leader of the local Women's Political Council (WPC). This group helped organize the Montgomery bus boycott. Robinson made desegregating the city buses a top priority. She was arrested several times. A cop threw a stone through her window. Another cop poured acid on her car. Dr. Martin Luther King Jr. said, "[Robinson], perhaps more than any other person, was active on every level of the protest." Robinson wrote a book about her life in 1987. She moved to Los Angeles, California, and died in 1992.

Vocabulary
opponent (uh-POH-nuhnt)
someone who is against something

FLASH FACT!
E. D. Nixon was an important African American civil rights activist. He played a key role in planning the boycott.

ACT 1

NARRATOR: *It's December 1, 1955.* **REGINALD BROWN** *and* **LOUIS WASHBURN** *are talking. They're in Reginald's church.*

LOUIS: Today was a big day. Rosa Parks stood up for all of us.

REGINALD: What did she do?

LOUIS: She **rebelled** against the bus system.

REGINALD: It's about time. It's not fair how our buses are segregated. I've never liked how African Americans can only sit in the back rows of the bus.

LOUIS: It's also not fair how we have to get up and stand if white people want our seats. We pay for the seats just like they do.

REGINALD: So, tell me what Rosa did.

LOUIS: She sat in a seat toward the back of a full bus. Then, a white person came on.

Vocabulary
rebelled (rih-BELD)
rose up in opposition

FLASH FACT!
Rosa Parks was arrested and fined $10 for refusing to get out of her seat. That's almost $100 in today's money.

REGINALD: Did the bus driver ask her to give up her seat?

LOUIS: He sure did. But she refused!

REGINALD: Was she arrested?

LOUIS: She sure was! But we have a plan.

REGINALD: A plan?

LOUIS: She's working with other civil rights leaders like myself. We're planning a big boycott. Rosa is the perfect **heroine** for our cause.

REGINALD: We need justice. Church leaders like myself are ready to help! Let me know what we can do.

LOUIS: As a leader of the church, you have a lot of influence. We need you to help spread the word. We need to boycott the city buses. Tell African Americans to not ride the bus anymore.

Vocabulary
heroine (HER-oh-in) female hero

FLASH FACT!
Church leaders sent out many posters and notices. They supported the boycott.

REGINALD: That sounds like a great idea. Over 75 percent of the bus riders are African Americans. If we stop riding the buses, then the city will lose money.

LOUIS: We need to send a message. We need to let the people in power know that we matter.

REGINALD: You can count on me.

NARRATOR: MATILDA LEE *owns a fabric store.* **ROSA PARKS** *is a seamstress. Rosa shops at Matilda's store. Rosa and Matilda are talking at her store.*

ROSA: How are you doing today, Matilda?

MATILDA: I'm great, Rosa. But I heard you got arrested yesterday. Are you okay?

ROSA: I'm fine with the arrest. My friends **bailed** me out. But I'm not fine with what's been happening to me and my fellow African Americans.

LOCATION SHOOTING
REAL-WORLD SETTING

Troy University is in Montgomery, Alabama. University officials wanted to build a parking garage. But they saw people standing on the corner. People stopped to read a sign about Rosa Parks. It was at that corner that Parks refused to give up her seat. University officials decided the corner was too important for a parking garage. They built a library and museum dedicated to Parks. The museum and library opened on December 1, 2000. This was the anniversary of the day she refused to give up her seat. The Rosa Parks Museum is on the first floor. It has a lot of information about the Montgomery bus boycott. It has exhibits. It has artifacts. It has programs and activities. The museum also has a bus. It's not the bus that Parks sat on. But it looks like that bus.

Vocabulary
bailed (BAYLD) paid money to release someone from custody

FLASH FACT!
The boycott leaders were punished for interfering with businesses.

MATILDA: What do you mean?

ROSA: We're not treated equally. We have separate schools. We have separate bathrooms. We have separate pools. We have separate restaurants. We have separate seating **sections** on the bus.

MATILDA: Why is that a bad thing?

ROSA: We're all Americans. I pay taxes just like you do. I'm a human being just like you. I should be treated in the same way.

Vocabulary

sections (SEK-shuhnz) special areas

racism (RAY-siz-uhm) a system of discrimination against people of a different race

FLASH FACT!

Many whites in Montgomery wanted to keep the city segregated.

MATILDA: But this is Alabama. We've got a proud tradition of separating the races.

ROSA: That's not a tradition. That's **racism**.

MATILDA: I don't understand. It's just the way we've been doing things. It's been fine so far.

ROSA: It's been fine for you. But it's not fine for me.

NARRATOR: **REGINALD BROWN** *and* **ROSA PARKS** *are talking before they meet others. It's December 5. Tonight is the first meeting of the Montgomery Improvement Association. Dr. Martin Luther King Jr. will be speaking. They're planning a boycott.*

REGINALD: Are you ready for tonight's meeting?

ROSA: It's exciting to have so many of our community's leaders in one place. It feels like we're on to something big.

REGINALD: Your bravery set all this in motion.

ROSA: There were other brave souls before me. And there will be many more brave souls in the future. We need as many people as possible to fight for freedom.

REGINALD: We're expecting over 7,000 people at the church tonight. All of our church meetings have been **packed**.

ROSA: People want change.

Vocabulary
packed (PAKD) full of people

FLASH FACT!
Dr. Martin Luther King Jr. was one of the main leaders of the civil rights movement.

ACT 2

NARRATOR: *The boycott has started.* **REGINALD BROWN** *and* **LOUIS WASHBURN** *discuss its success.*

LOUIS: I can't thank you enough for everything you're doing.

REGINALD: We've had our hands full. It's been quite busy around here.

LOUIS: I heard that over 90 percent of Montgomery residents are refusing to ride the buses. How do you keep your church members motivated?

REGINALD: We host many meetings. We try to keep people's spirits up. We remind them we're fighting for equality.

LOUIS: Meetings are a good idea. It's good to remember that we're all in this together.

REGINALD: We've also been helping people get where they need to go without buses.

LOUIS: That's been the biggest problem with the boycott. People need **alternative transportation**.

Vocabulary
alternative (awl-TUR-nuh-tiv)
different

transportation
(trans-pur-TAY-shuhn) a way
of getting somewhere like cars,
buses, trains, or planes

FLASH FACT!
*Some African Americans
rode bicycles instead
of the bus.*

REGINALD: Boycotting buses is not easy. People have to get to work or they'll lose their jobs.

LOUIS: What have you done to help?

REGINALD: I find people who **volunteer** their cars and time. I coordinate ride shares. Luckily, many of our church members have stepped up. They pick up people from their homes. They pick up people from work.

LOUIS: That's great. What else? I want to share your good ideas with others.

REGINALD: Some of our members walk instead of ride the bus. They've worn out their shoes.

LOUIS: Is it dangerous for them? Other church leaders have told me that white people have yelled terrible things to our walkers.

REGINALD: We have the same problem. I created a buddy system. People walk together.

Vocabulary
volunteer (vah-luhn-TEER)
to freely offer to do something

FLASH FACT!
African Americans faced setbacks and violence during the boycott. They continued to stand together and avoid the buses.

LOUIS: It's so important to have community. Many people lost faith when Dr. King's house got bombed. Some quit.

REGINALD: If not for the church, people would've gotten more scared. I'm very proud.

LOUIS: We're living out our belief that all people are created equal.

REGINALD: We'll keep organizing and fighting until we get **dignity** and justice.

Vocabulary
dignity (DIG-nih-tee) the state of being worthy of honor or respect

FLASH FACT!
During the boycott, Montgomery buses were sometimes nearly empty.

NARRATOR: **ROSA PARKS** *and* **MATILDA LEE** *are talking at Matilda's store. Matilda is frustrated. Her business is losing money.*

MATILDA: This boycott has been going on for a long time. This is not good for my business.

ROSA: We used to ride the buses downtown to shop. But, because of the boycott, we don't come down here anymore. We're also boycotting white-owned businesses.

MATILDA: I've lost a lot of money. My uncle works for the city bus company. He said they're losing a lot of money too.

ROSA: I heard the mayor asked white people to ride the buses.

MATILDA: He did. But it didn't work. The bus company had to raise their **fares**.

ROSA: We'll keep boycotting until we get what we want.

MATILDA: What do you want?

ROSA: We want to be treated politely. We want seating to be first come, first served. We want African Americans to be hired as drivers.

NARRATOR: *It's December 1956. A year has passed.* **LOUIS WASHBURN** *and* **ROSA PARKS** *are talking.*

LOUIS: I can't believe this boycott is almost over.

BLOOPERS
HISTORICAL MISTAKES

Many people think Rosa Parks refused to give up her seat because she was tired. This is not true. She wanted to make a statement. Parks was a civil rights activist. Activists fight for change. She broke the law on purpose. She wanted to inspire people to fight for civil rights. She was a leader in the Montgomery chapter of the National Association for the Advancement of Colored People. Parks is described as "quiet." But she calls herself a rebel. There's a Rosa Parks Collection at the Library of Congress in Washington, D.C. It features her personal writings, letters, speech notes, records, and photographs. This collection proves that Parks is a freedom fighter. She wrote, "I had been pushed around all my life and felt at this moment that I couldn't take it anymore."

Vocabulary
fares (FAIRZ) the money a passenger on public transportation has to pay

FLASH FACT!
King and other African Americans rode in the front of the bus after the boycott.

27

ROSA: We've proved that we matter. We've shown everyone that we're powerful. More importantly, we've proved to ourselves that we're capable.

LOUIS: This is only the start. The road to freedom is long and bumpy.

ROSA: There's much more work to be done. The forces of **oppression** are strong. Opponents are attacking our cars. They're attacking our homes. They're yelling ugly things at us.

LOUIS: The **Ku Klux Klan** is growing. They try to scare us. They're throwing more bombs. They're burning crosses.

ROSA: We don't scare so easily. And we can do the work. If we won in Montgomery, we'll win in other places.

LOUIS: We're an army of freedom fighters. We shall overcome.

Vocabulary

oppression (uh-PRESH-uhn)
prolonged cruel or unjust treatment
by people in power

Ku Klux Klan (KOO KLUKS KLAN)
an organization that promotes
white supremacy and is known
for violent actions against
African Americans

FLASH FACT!

*Civil rights leaders
celebrate their victory
in Montgomery.*

EVENT TIMELINE

March 1954: The WPC meets with W. A. Gayle. Gayle is the mayor of Montgomery, Alabama. The WPC recommends changes for the Montgomery bus system.

May 17, 1954: The U.S. Supreme Court ends segregation in schools. Prior to this, African American and white students had to go to different schools.

March 2, 1955: Claudette Colvin is arrested for not giving up her bus seat. African American leaders in Montgomery meet with city officials.

December 1, 1955: Rosa Parks refuses to give up her seat. She is arrested.

December 2, 1955: The WPC calls for a single-day boycott on December 5.

December 5, 1955: Over 90 percent of the African American community in Montgomery participates in the boycott. African American leaders meet to extend the boycott. The MIA is created.

December 8, 1955: The MIA makes a formal list of demands. The city refuses to comply.

December 13, 1955: The MIA organizes a car pool system.

January 30, 1956: Dr. Martin Luther King Jr.'s home is bombed. He calls for a peaceful protest.

June 5, 1956: A federal district court rules that bus segregation is illegal.

November 13, 1956: The Supreme Court upholds the district ruling.

December 20, 1956: The Supreme Court's ruling is delivered to Montgomery City Hall. The boycott is over.

December 21, 1956: Montgomery's city buses are desegregated.

CONSIDER THIS!

TAKE A POSITION! Learn about the civil rights movement. Some say the Montgomery bus boycott sparked the movement. Do you agree or disagree? Argue your point with reasons and evidence.

SAY WHAT? James F. Blake was the bus driver who told Rosa Parks to give up her seat. He said, "I wasn't trying to do anything to that Parks woman except do my job. She was in violation of the city codes. So what was I supposed to do?" What do you think about Blake's decision? Explain what you would have done if you were him.

THINK ABOUT IT! Have you ever ridden on a public bus? What are the pros and cons of public buses?

Learn More

Gitlin, Marty. *The Montgomery Bus Boycott.* Ann Arbor, MI: Cherry Lake Publishing, 2014.

Llanas, Sheila. *Children in the Civil Rights Era.* Lake Elmo, MN: Focus Readers, 2019.

McCormick, Anita Louise. *Rosa Parks and the Montgomery Bus Boycott.* New York, NY: Rosen Publishing Group, 2018.

INDEX

ABOUT THE AUTHOR

Dr. Virginia Loh-Hagan is an author, university professor, and former classroom teacher. She's never been to Alabama. But she's been to Nashville, Tennessee. She ate at Woolworth on 5th. This is where the February 1960 lunch counter sit-ins took place. She lives in San Diego with her very tall husband and very naughty dogs. To learn more about her, visit www.virginialoh.com.